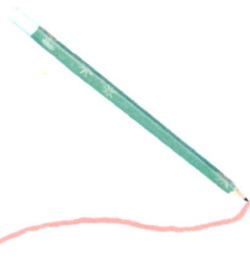

LENSES OF LIFE

First edition published June 2023

Text copyright: Dave Acton
Illustration copyright: Brenda Muñoz

ISBN 978-0-6458310-0-9

lensesoflife.com
lensesoflifebook

LENSES OF LIFE

A collection of inspirational rhymes for
experiencing magic in the everyday

CONTENTS

LENSES OF LIFE

The lenses through which we choose to see,
can bring in to focus a new way to be.

The way we use and focus our attention,
can shift our beliefs and change our perception.

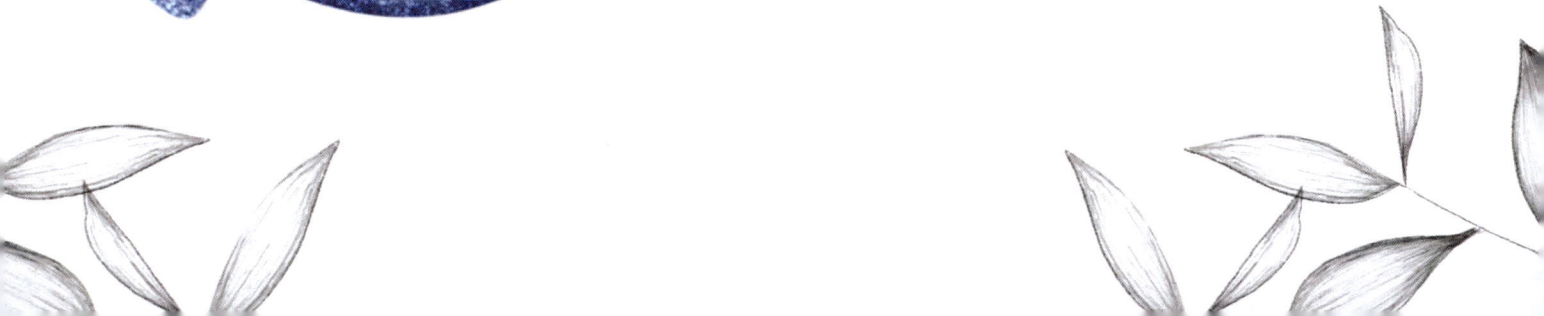

ARMCHAIR OF APPRECIATION

I woke up this morning with a grateful heart,
and said thanks to my bed for a good morning start.

I thanked the water as it flowed on my head,
and bowed to the clouds, up overhead.

I waved to the birds as they soared through the sky,
and admired my art with a gleam in my eye.

I smiled at my cat, curled up in a ball,
sat in my armchair, I felt content, after all.

I breathed in fresh air, and felt so alive,
I was aware right now, I had so much to thrive.

Today, I feel happy, I have enough,
today, I feel grateful, for all the simple stuff.

Save Me

BACKPACK OF BELIEF

When you're called to adventure, near or far,
your dreams can come true, whatever they are.

Just put on your backpack of belief,
and of your life, you can be the chief.

If you're doubting your ability,
trust in possibility.

Whisper proudly, "I can do it."
with belief, there's nothing to it."

BICYCLE OF BALANCE

One day, my friend asked me, "What is balance?"
I said, "It's worth developing as one of your talents."

"But I thought that balance was a mysterious thing,
like the force or yin yang from the Tao Te Ching?"

"That may be so, but for me, it's more simple,
I think that a bike is an appropriate symbol.

When you're riding a bike, you're up and you're down,
you're left and you're right, you might smile and frown.

It's the little adjustments that keep you on track,
it might take some time, but you'll get the knack."

"So next time I'm pedalling up a great big hill,
I could balance that effort with some downwards chill?"

"Exactly, my friend you can yang and you can yin,
and as you ride, you'll find balance within."

COAT OF COMPASSION

My favourite coat is always in fashion,
it's cosy and warm, it's my coat of compassion.

If someone's in need of understanding and care,
I just put it right on and pull up a chair.

And when my listening is done and they're feeling much better,
I place my coat on their shoulders and hand them a letter.

"You are brave, you are worthy, you are loved and enough,
you are safe and resilient when times seem tough,

You are smart and important and your purpose is clear,
I'm grateful to know you and be with you here."

HAT OF HUMOUR

There's a funny guy who lives in a nearby town,
some people say he's just a big clown.

But research is revealing the power of a laugh,
and you can plot the benefits on a statistical graph.

Science is proving that some laughter each day,
improves happiness and well-being each time that you play.

But the funny guy nearby already knew that,
'cause each time he puts on his humorous hat,

The laughter and squeals of playful delight,
leave everyone feeling happy and bright.

KITE of KINDNESS

I looked up and saw something up high,
a kite of kindness flew up in the sky.

Its colours were friendly and it danced with the breeze,
it made me feel welcome and much more at ease.

I waved to its owner and she beckoned me closer,
"Would you like to try, it's easy to fly."

So she passed me the line and it felt truly sublime,
to see the kite dance around and watch the kindness compound.

As others approached, we gently coached,
and as they flew the kite, our kindness took flight.

MUG OF MINDFULNESS

I start my day with a mug of tea,
it's a ritual I love which nourishes me.

To me, the tea is a chance each day,
to let past and future drift away.

It's just me in the kitchen with a boiling pot,
the bubbling and whistling as the water gets hot.

The smell of fresh tea as I scoop it in,
and I patiently wait and let the brewing begin.

I've arrived in this moment, mindful and clear,
and it's a gift indeed to simply be here.

As I raise my mug up to my lips,
I feel the warmth on my hands as I take a few sips.

Then I sit myself down in a cosy place,
with my mug of tea and a smile on my face.

PATH OF PRESENCE

I took a long walk the other day,
along a path where I could hear kids play.

Where I could hear the ocean's rhythmic sound,
and smell waffle cones baking in the nearby town.

I could see people relaxing on their colourful chairs,
some by themselves and some were in pairs.

The children laughed and built castles of sand,
I approached the water and dipped in my hand.

Palm trees were swaying high up above,
a couple passed by who were dearly in love.

A group of old fellas chatted in their spot,
they were discussing again how it was ever so hot.

My mind was right there, clear and awake,
on that path of presence I'm grateful to take.

PLANT OF PATIENCE

We planted a fruit seed ten years ago,
we watered and nurtured, and it started to grow.

As we patiently waited, it grew branches and leaves,
it's amazing to watch seeds turn into trees.

Now I sit in the shade of this wonderful tree,
enjoying the fruit it provided for me.

It all began from that seed so small,
and with our patience and care, it now stands tall.

RUG OF RELAXATION

We went for a picnic at the start of spring,
the flowers were blooming and we could hear the birds sing.

We laid out our rug at the grassy green park,
and we stayed there all day until it almost got dark.

We saw shapes in the clouds as they drifted on by,
and we nibbled on fruit and relaxed with a sigh.

We leisurely strolled to the edge of the lake,
then returned to our rug for a small piece of cake.

The contentment I felt was like floating on air,
as I felt the spring breeze flow through my hair.

Then we decided to nap in the afternoon shade,
relaxed on our rug in the park where we laid.

SURFBOARD OF SERENITY

Sliding and gliding on water so clear,
on top of your surfboard with nothing to fear.

Salt water spraying, cool mist on your face,
a new wave is forming and you're quick to embrace.

Now standing and riding the curved wall of sea,
your surfboard of serenity has filled you with glee.

You lean back, you lean forward, balancing with ease,
dolphins surf with you through aquamarine seas.

And in this moment, you feel totally free,
like time has stood still and it's all meant to be.

And back on the shore, you look out at the ocean,
you smile and bow to the waves and their motion.

WINDOW OF WONDER

Moonlight streams in through my window at night,
the sky full of stars such an awesome sight.

The planets in our solar system,
our heroes and teachers who impart their wisdom.

Our Milky Way Galaxy,
our path to truth from fallacy.

Our rover on Mars, "Curiosity",
universal grandiosity.

I imagine the future ahead of me,
and the wondrous changes I will see.

Now reusable rockets and electric cars,
next vacations in space and homes on Mars.

Expeditions to Saturn's moon,
a long time away or could it be soon?

Whatever happens, I know right now,
that when I look up, I just think "Wow."

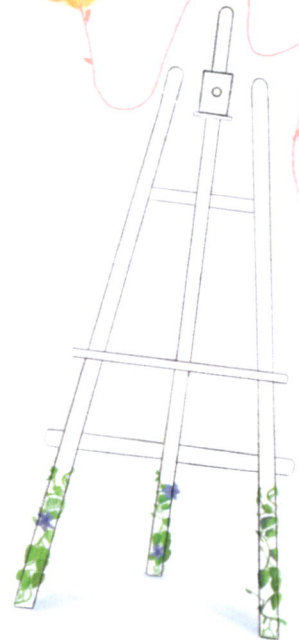

ABOUT THE AUTHOR & ILLUSTRATOR

Dave Acton is a designer from the Sunshine Coast of Australia. In 'Lenses of Life,' his first book, he combines his love for simple rhymes with important life values. What started as a personal project has grown into a collection that he hopes will speak to others. When he's not busy with design work or writing, Dave enjoys exploring the world through his camera lens, walking his two Chihuahuas, and taking in the beauty of the Australian coastline.

Brenda Muñoz, a self-taught digital artist and illustrator from Colombia now in Western Australia, brings years of experience to her vibrant compositions. 'Lenses of Life' marks her debut as a book illustrator, a milestone she's excited to share. Brenda's primary focus is on crafting illustrations from real-life scenarios using digital painting and traditional media such as graphite, watercolours, and pastels. She continually refines her artistic skills, motivated by this new chapter in her creative journey.

Dave and Brenda would like to express their deepest gratitude to their friends, partners, teachers and family who have provided belief, kindness, and patience in the creation of 'Lenses of Life.' Each of you has contributed to this journey in your unique way, and for that, we are truly thankful.

Above all, we want to thank you, the reader. Your support and interest in this book means more than words can express and encourages us to keep creating.

Thank you.

www.ingramcontent.com/pod-product-compliance
Lightning Source LLC
Chambersburg PA
CBRC100736150426
42811CB00070B/1910